THE STANLEY CUP

by Shane Frederick

CAPSTONE PRESS
a capstone imprint

Capstone Captivate is published by Capstone Press,
1710 Roe Crest Drive, North Mankato, Minnesota, 56003.
www.capstonepub.com

Copyright © 2019 by Capstone Press, a Capstone imprint. All rights reserved. No part of this publication may be reproduced in whole or in part, or stored in a retrieval system, or transmitted in any form or by any means, electronic, mechanical, photocopying, recording, or otherwise, without written permission of the publisher.

Library of Congress Cataloging-in-Publication Data is available on the Library of Congress website.
ISBN: 978-1-5435-9196-5 (hardcover)
ISBN: 978-1-4966-5785-5 (paperback)
ISBN: 978-1-5435-9202-3 (eBook PDF)

Summary:
Discover the surprising facts, amazing stories, and legendary players of the Stanley Cup.

Image Credits
Associated Press: A.E. Maloof, 27, Charles Krupa, 24, Jeff Roberson, cover; Dreamstime: Jenta Wong, 20, Jerry Coli, 10, 13, 19; Getty Images: Bruce Bennett, 15, Transcendental Graphics, 7, 11; Newscom: Cal Sport Media/John Crouch, 5, Icon SMI/IHA, 17, Icon SMI/John McDonough, 16, Icon SMI/Kathleen Hinkel, 23, Icon SMI/Rich Kane, 21, Reuters/Gary Hershorn, 18, 29, USA Today Sports/Jerry Lai, 9 (top), ZUMA Press/Joel Marklund, 9 (bottom); Shutterstock: Adam Vilimek, 1

Design Elements: Shutterstock

Editorial Credits
Editor: Gena Chester; Designer: Sarah Bennett; Media Researcher: Eric Gohl; Production Specialist: Spencer Rosio

All internet sites appearing in back matter were available and accurate when this book was sent to press.

Printed and bound in the USA
3162

Table of Contents

CHAPTER 1
It's All about the Cup 4

CHAPTER 2
The Teams 8

CHAPTER 3
The Players 14

CHAPTER 4
The Moments 22

Glossary 30
Read More 31
Internet Sites 31
Index 32

Words that are in **bold** can be found in the glossary.

CHAPTER 1

It's All about the Cup

For 12 years, Alex Ovechkin was one of the best players in the National Hockey **League** (NHL). He helped the Washington Capitals become one of the best teams in the league. But something was missing. The Capitals hadn't yet won a Stanley Cup.

In 2018, which was Ovechkin's 13th season, the Capitals beat the Vegas Golden Knights to win the championship. Ovechkin screamed with excitement when he held the Stanley Cup.

Fast Fact!
Twice, the Stanley Cup was not awarded. The first time was in 1919 because of a flu outbreak. The second was in 2005. That year the full NHL season was canceled due to a dispute between players and team owners.

Alex Ovechkin holds up the Stanley Cup.

The Oldest Trophy

Winning a championship is great in any sport. But in the NHL, it's a little more special. The winning team gets the oldest trophy in **professional** sports in North America—the Stanley Cup. It's even older than the NHL! Hockey teams first played for the trophy in 1893. A team from Canada called the Montreal **Amateur** Athletic Association won it the first two times.

The trophy traveled back and forth to different teams across North America for many years before it finally became the NHL's championship trophy. The Stanley Cup is a difficult trophy to win. After a long, 82-game **regular season**, eight teams from each **conference** make the **playoffs**. Each round of the playoffs is a best-of-seven series. This means a team must win four games before moving on to the next round.

The Ottawa hockey team poses with the Stanley Cup. Ottawa got the Cup for winning their 1906 league championship. The Cup was first awarded by the NHL in 1918.

World Tour

Every summer after the Stanley Cup Final, each player from the winning team gets to have the trophy for one day. Players have taken the Stanley Cup to their hometowns and other special places around the world for parties and parades. The Cup has been to 25 different countries over the years.

CHAPTER 2

The Teams

The Pittsburgh Penguins

One of the hardest things to do in the NHL is to win two championships in a row. But the Pittsburgh Penguins did it. They won the Stanley Cup in 2016 and 2017. It was the first time a team won back-to-back Cups in almost 20 years!

The Penguins were a high-scoring team during those seasons. Star center Sidney Crosby led the way, but he didn't do it alone. Evgeni Malkin and Phil Kessel also pushed Pittsburgh's powerful **offense**. Goalies Matt Murray and Marc-André Fleury did their best to stop the other teams from scoring.

Fast Fact!

The Penguins also won back-to-back Stanley Cups in 1991 and 1992. Mario Lemieux scored a total of 32 goals and had 46 **assists** in 40 playoff games over the two seasons.

Penguins right wing Patric Hornqvist (left) shoots the puck past Predators goalie Pekka Rinne.

The Penguins celebrate their second Cup win in a row.

Montreal Canadiens goalie Ken Dryden helped the Canadiens win the Stanley Cup six times.

The Montreal Canadiens

No team has won more NHL championships than the Montreal Canadiens. They have won the Stanley Cup 24 times.

From 1956 to 1960, Montreal won five Stanley Cups in a row. From 1965 to 1969, the Canadiens won four out of five tries. Three players were important to all nine of those championships. They were centers Jean Beliveau and Henri Richard and winger Claude Provost.

Jean Béliveau (right) holds the Stanley Cup with teammate Maurice Richard.

During a third run between 1976 and 1979, they won another four championships in a row. The 1976–77 team might have been their best ever. Montreal had a **record** of 60 wins, 8 losses, and 12 ties in the regular season. They lost only two games in the playoffs. They swept the Boston Bruins in the final series.

The New York Islanders

After the Canadiens' run in the 1970s ended, the New York Islanders took over. They became the team nobody could beat for four years in a row.

The Islanders won the Stanley Cup in 1980, 1981, 1982, and 1983. Four different teams had shots to take the trophy away from them. But they were no match for forwards Bryan Trottier and Mike Bossy, defenseman Denis Potvin, and goalie Billy Smith.

The Islanders made it to the Final in 1984 too. But they lost to the Edmonton Oilers.

Clark Gillies holds the Stanley Cup as he and teammates celebrate their 1980 Final win over the Philadelphia Flyers.

CHAPTER 3

The Players

The Rockets

After a team wins the Stanley Cup, the names of the players get put on the trophy. Over 100 years ago in 1907, the Montreal Wanderers were the first team to put names on the Cup. Coaches and other team members get their names on it too. Fifty players have their name on the Cup at least five times.

Maurice Richards was known as "Rocket." He was speedy and known as one of the all-time great goal scorers in NHL history. He led the Montreal Canadiens to eight Stanley Cup wins. Henri Richard, his younger and smaller brother, was called "Pocket Rocket." The younger brother helped the Canadiens win 11 times.

Fast Fact!

Jean Béliveau has his name on the Stanley Cup more than any other person. He helped the Canadiens win 10 times as a player and seven more times as a team executive.

Henri Richard warms up on the ice in 1972. He played with the Montreal Canadiens for 20 years.

Edmonton Oilers player Wayne Gretzky waits for the puck during a game against the Los Angeles Kings.

Wayne Gretzky

Wayne Gretzky was known as "The Great One." He scored more goals, assists, and **points** than any player in NHL history. His name made the Cup four times.

During the 1985 playoffs, Gretzky outdid his competition. He had 17 goals and 30 assists. He helped get the Oilers their second championship. Gretzky led the Oilers to back-to-back championships again in 1987 and 1988. In the 1988 Final against the Bruins, Gretzky had 13 points in five games. He scored three goals and assisted on 10 others.

Wayne Gretzky played for four teams throughout his 20 seasons in the NHL.

Patrick Roy

The Conn Smythe Trophy is awarded to the best player in the Stanley Cup playoffs. Sometimes it goes to the player who scores the most goals or racks up the most points. But goalies often win the award as well.

Goalie Patrick Roy is the only player to win the Conn Smythe as the playoffs' most valuable player three times. He won it twice with the Canadiens in 1986 and 1993. He won it again in 2001 with the Colorado Avalanche. He didn't let in any goals in four games. Two of those games were in the final series against the New Jersey Devils. Roy's skill also helped the Avalanche win the Stanley Cup in 1996.

Patrick Roy wins the Conn Smyth Trophy in the 2001 Stanley Cup Final. Roy is the only player to win the award three times.

Canadiens goalie Patrick Roy makes a save against the Calgary Flames.

Fast Fact!

In 1928, New York Rangers coach Lester Patrick had to suit up as the team's goalie because the starter got hurt. He was 44 years old, and it was the only NHL game he ever played in. The Rangers won and went on to win the Cup.

Los Angeles Kings goalie Jonathan Quick

Jonathan Quick

The 2012 Los Angeles Kings weren't expected to go far in the Stanley Cup playoffs. They were the second-lowest scoring team in the NHL during the regular season.

Once they got in the playoffs, though, goaltender Jonathan Quick turned into a brick wall. Quick played in all 20 playoff games. In those 20 games, the Kings won 16 and lost only 4. He had three **shutouts** and allowed an average of 1.41 goals per game.

In the six-game final against the New Jersey Devils, the Kings outscored the Devils 16–8. Only seven pucks got by Quick. He won the Conn Smythe Trophy. The surprising Kings won the Stanley Cup.

Jonathan Quick blocks a shot from New Jersey Devils player Dainius Zubrus.

CHAPTER 4

The Moments

Game 7 Thrills

There is nothing more exciting than a Game 7 in the Stanley Cup Final. It all comes down to one game to decide a championship.

A Game 7 has decided the Stanley Cup winner 16 times in NHL history. In 2011, the Boston Bruins defeated the Vancouver Canucks 4–0 in Game 7. Bruins goalie Tim Thomas stopped 37 shots. The Bruins had another chance in 2019. During Game 7 this time, St. Louis Blues rookie goalie Jordan Binnington was the hero. He stopped 32 shots in a 4–1 victory. The Bruins lost. The Blues won their first-ever Stanley Cup.

Two Game 7s have gone into overtime. The Detroit Red Wings won both times, once in 1950 and again in 1954.

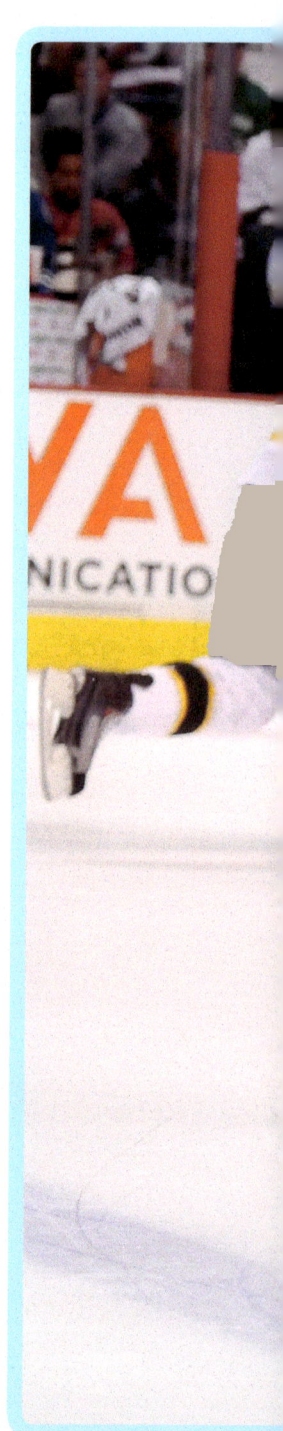

Boston Bruins center Gregory Campbell (left) beats Vancouver Canucks player Manny Malhotra to the puck in Game 7 in 2011.

Edmonton Oilers goalie Bill Ranford kicks the puck away from the net during Game 1 of the 1990 Stanley Cup Final. The Oilers went on to beat the Bruins 3–2 in overtime.

Up All Night

In the NHL regular season, tied games are decided by a five-minute overtime. The first team to score wins. If no goal is scored, the teams go to a shootout to decide the winner. But in the Stanley Cup playoffs, overtime periods last 20 minutes. Teams keep playing until someone scores a goal. The longest games in NHL history are playoff games.

The longest game ever came in a semifinal series between the Detroit Red Wings and Montreal Maroons in 1936. It needed six overtimes to finish. Detroit won 1–0. Rookie Modere "Mud" Bruneteau finally scored the goal at 2:25 a.m.

The longest game in a final series was Game 1 between the Oilers and Bruins in 1990. The Oilers had traded Wayne Gretzky and had something to prove. The Oilers' Petr Klima scored in the third overtime period for a 3–2 victory. Klima didn't play much in that game, but he came up big in the end. The Oilers ended up defeating the Bruins four games to one.

Super Shot

Bobby Orr changed the way a defenseman played. Many thought he was the best defenseman ever. The Bruins star wasn't afraid to leave his spot at the blue line to take the puck to the net to score goals. That's what Orr did in overtime of Game 4 in the 1970 Stanley Cup Final.

The Bruins were playing the St. Louis Blues. They had won the first three games. The Blues weren't going to go away quietly, though. The game was tied 3–3 at the end of regulation.

In the first minute of overtime, Orr passed to teammate Derek Sanderson. Sanderson passed it back as Orr raced to the front of the net. Orr shot the puck past the goalie. He flew through the air like Superman to celebrate. The Bruins won 4–3 for their first championship since 1941.

Strange Tradition

Even the fans have their moments during the Stanley Cup playoffs. In Detroit, fans throw an octopus onto the ice. It first happened in 1952. The animal's eight legs represented the number of games the Red Wings, their home team, needed to win the Stanley Cup. Nowadays, teams need to win a total of 16 games over four series, but the tradition continues.

Bruins player Bobby Orr flies through the air to celebrate his goal against the St. Louis Blues.

What Just Happened?

Teams always celebrate an overtime goal, especially during a Stanley Cup game. But it took a few seconds for the Chicago Blackhawks to celebrate an overtime goal that won the championship in 2010.

The Blackhawks and Philadelphia Flyers were tied 3–3. The Blackhawks' Patrick Kane skated the puck along the boards and down to the goal line. He fired a shot that he didn't think would go in. Somehow, the puck found its way through goalie Michael Leighton. Hardly anyone realized the puck was in the net. After the play was reviewed, the celebration was on.

"What a feeling. I can't believe it. We just won the Stanley Cup. I can't believe this just happened. . . . It's something you dream about, scoring the final goal in the Stanley Cup finals," Kane said.

The Chicago Blackhawks surround Patrick Kane after his winning goal.

Glossary

amateur (AM-uh-chur)—describes a sports league that athletes take part in for fun instead of for money

assist (uh-SIST)—a pass that leads to a score by a teammate

conference (KAHN-fuhr-uhns)—a grouping of sports teams that play against each other within a league

league (LEEG)—a group of sports teams that play against each other

offense (aw-FENSS)—the team that has the puck and is trying to score

playoff (PLAY-awf)—a series of games played after the regular season to decide a championship

point (POINT)—any goal or assist that is part of a player's scoring total

professional (pruh-FESH-uh-nuhl)—a person who makes money by doing something other people do for fun, such as playing ice hockey

record (REK-urd)—when something is done better than anyone has ever done it before

regular season (reg-yuh-LUR SEE-zuhn)—the normal set of games that teams play in a year

shutout (SHUHT-out)—when a team doesn't score

Read More

Doeden, Matt. *The Stanley Cup Playoffs: The Quest for Hockey's Biggest Prize*. Minneapolis, MN: Millbrook Press, 2020.

Omoth, Tyler. *A Superfan's Guide to Pro Hockey Teams*. North Mankato, MN: Capstone Press, 2018.

Zweig, Eric. *Stanley Cup: The Complete History*. Buffalo, NY: Firefly Books Inc., 2018.

Internet Sites

Hockey Hall of Fame
www.hhof.com

Hockey Reference
www.hockey-reference.com

NHL Official Website
www.nhl.com

Index

awards, 18, 21

Boston Bruins, 11, 17, 22, 25
    Orr, Bobby, 26
    Sanderson, Derek, 26
    Thomas, Tim, 22

Chicago Blackhawks, 28
    Kane, Patrick, 28
Colorado Avalanche
    Roy, Patrick, 18

Detroit Red Wings, 22, 25, 27
    Bruneteau, Modere, 25

Edmonton Oilers, 12, 25
    Gretzky, Wayne, 17, 25
    Klima, Petr, 25

Los Angeles Kings, 21
    Quick, Jonathan, 21

Montreal Amateur Athletic Association, 6
Montreal Canadiens, 11
    Béliveau, Jean, 11, 15
    Provost, Claude, 11
    Richard, Henri, 11, 14
    Richards, Maurice, 14
    Roy, Patrick, 18
Montreal Maroons, 25
Montreal Wanderers, 14

New Jersey Devils, 18, 21
New York Islanders, 12
    Bossy, Mike, 12
    Potvin, Denis, 12
    Smith, Billy, 12
    Trottier, Bryan, 12
New York Rangers
    Patrick, Lester, 19

overtime periods, 25, 26, 28

Philadelphia Flyers, 28
    Leighton, Michael, 28
Pittsburgh Penguins, 8
    Crosby, Sidney, 8
    Fleury, Marc-André, 8
    Kessel, Phil, 8
    Lemieux, Mario, 8
    Malkin, Evgeni, 8
    Murray, Matt, 8

records, 11, 15, 17

shutouts, 21
St. Louis Blues, 22, 26
    Binnington, Jordan, 22

Vancouver Canucks, 22
Vegas Golden Knights, 4

Washington Capitals
    Ovechkin, Alex, 4